MESSAGES IN A BOTTLE:
COMMUNICATIONS TO MY FUTURE SELF

The Poetry of Michael Graves

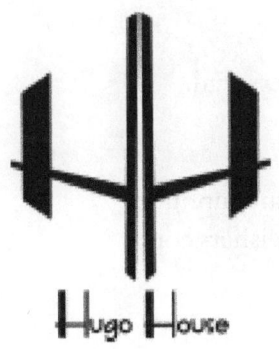

Messages in a Bottle: Communications to My Future Self

©2017 Michael Graves. All Rights Reserved.

No part of this book may be reproduced or transmitted in any form or by any means, electronic or mechanical, including photocopying, recording, or by any information storage and retrieval system without written permission of the publisher.

ISBN: 9781936449781

Cover Art : Dali Bahat
Cover and Interior: Christa E. Kegl

Hugo House Publishers, Ltd.
Denver, Colorado
Austin, Texas
Banyan Tree Press is an imprint of
www.HugoHousePublishers.com

This book is dedicated to Holley, and to those who have helped. To those who move forward when the times call for it instead of hanging back. And to those with the integrity to say what needs to be said and to do what needs to be done; regardless of consequence. It is upon these individuals that the future of everything rests.

My deepest gratitude goes to Bennett Fontenot, DDS, yet again, without whose help and generous support it would have taken far longer to get this book published. And to Patricia Ross and George Gluchowski at Hugo House. I could not have done it without you guys.

Cover designed by Dali Bahat. Thank you my friend for coming out of retirement once again, for this.

Contents

Dedication	iv
Beatitudes	9
A Movement in the Air	11
The View from the Lighthouse	12
The Life that you Create	15
The Belly of the Beast	16
Heroes (To Erin)	19
Runway 24 – Lukla, Nepal	20
The Mode of the Hummingbird	22
Dancing with the Muse	25
Darkness and Light	28
A Penchant for Strippers	30
I am not my chair	32
Why Are We Here?	35
Vengeance "lex talionis" (For the suicide bombers)	37
Dreams – (in four short acts)	39
This Moment in Time	42
Apparency	44
The Vengeance of Angels	46
Taking Off My Watch	47
Bricks	48
Circumstance	50
Authenticity	52
The Whisper of Sheets	53
Connecting Dots	55
Catch and Release	57
Mother is Listening	58

The Poet	60
Space	62
We should be more than just entertainment	64
Radiance	66
Integrity	68
Intention	69
Waiting for You	70
Life as a Human	73
Path	74
Borders is Closing	75
The Secret to Good Sex	77
The Perfect Life	79
Friendship	80
On the observation of a cripple – yet buoyant.	83
Different Doors	84
A Poet's Wish.	86
The Secret Handshake from God	87
The Taken Road	88
Weaver	89
The Easy Answer	92
Barriers to Flight	95
Why we do what we do	97
Actors	99
Barriers	100
Sailing – Song of the Daemons	103
Terrorist.	105
The Cliff	106
The Dance	108
Woman	110

The Root of Strength	112
A Simple Step	113
Quality	114
Spiderwebs and Evolution	115
Slicing Tomatoes	119
Tips From My Father	120
Thanksgiving	121
Decision	124
America 2197	126
Stardust	130
Maniac – For Syria	132
On Poetry and Social Responsibility	134
About the Author	140

MESSAGES IN A BOTTLE:
COMMUNICATIONS TO MY FUTURE SELF

Beatitudes

Blessed are those who refuse to fail
For they shall attain
impossible heights.

Blessed is the child who rides out life
alone, and blooms despite all.
for his is the resilience
of the unstoppable.

Blessed are those who give advice
and do not require that it be followed;
for they will be called friends.

Blessed are those who care enough to change conditions
where others will not.
For their lives, while perhaps more trying
will make the greatest difference.

Blessed are those who right the scales;
for their gift to the world
is sanity.

Blessed are those who follow Jerry Garcia and the boys.
For they shall be called "Deadheads*"
Wait... what?

Blessed are those who acknowledge and forgive the past.
For they will have
the clearest view of the future.

Blessed are those who grace the world with
new viewpoints, new games, and new vistas.
For theirs is the crown of creation.
And they will be the suppliers of dreams.

Blessed are those willing to honestly help
without hidden agenda;
for they will ease the burden.

Blessed are the defenders and healers of souls;
for they guard the route to eternity.

Blessed are those who understand the power of responsibility
and the fruitlessness of revenge.
For theirs will be the sanest perspective.

Blessed are those who strive to travel beyond the edge
of what is known.
For theirs is the uncharted realm.

Blessed are those who understand, and move forward
even under the most daunting conditions.
For they will forge the forward path.

And blessed are those who come back.
For some will call them angels.
And they will save
the world.

–Graves 1/28/11

Notes: *"Deadheads" is a term which was affectionately given to fans of the rock band "The Grateful Dead," which achieved iconic status in the 1970's. Jerry Garcia was the band's leader.

A Movement in the Air

Your future follows your choice.
Who you were
what you've done
what you've failed to do; mattered once.
Not now.

Your self-doubt
your second-guessing is baggage
that someone left behind to
clutter your life
in hopes that you might, at some future point
stumble over it in a darkened hallway, and upon
regaining your feet
choose a different path not your own.

Decide that your future is that of a hero
and it shall be.
Decide to allow yourself to fail
and that fate is yours.

You need no spells to grant permission
nor talismans. No contrivances of old.
You are permission.

You've always known that this is true.
You've felt it stirring
in your soul. A quiet disturbance.
An awareness in the back of your mind
like a movement in the air. Incessant
like the transit of the moon.

Your future is as you decide.

      –Graves 4/2/16

The View from the Lighthouse

I have seen the storms
far-off and approaching.
I have watched the crashing waves
yet to come
run their course.
I have heard the howling wind
in the dark wet night.

I have watched the tides.

I see the rocks that lie in wait
beneath the shiny surface
of the calm sea.
I see the slow
unstoppable
swell
of the tsunami
seeking
to subsume
the shoreline.

The sea itself is made of changes. Always
changes.

Some sudden and violent.
Some transient and fleeting.
Some deadly and permanent.

With perspective
you learn the difference.

Vicissitudes can kill you.
Even the word sounds like
choppy water.

Life can turn on a dime.
Let it.
Allow it to turn, and then
ride it
in your direction.

Anything else, and you founder
or become at last becalmed.

With perspective
you learn the difference.

Just because the water is choppy
does not mean
disaster is certain.
Adrift is not death.
It is simply

adrift.

Know the stable point of land.
Know the star that does not fail.
Know very well, the decision
that means more to you
than life.

And on that, plot your course.
And never

waver.

Do not panic
when the wind hits a fresh gale
when the waters turn angry
and the masts begin to creak and strain.
That is simply the way
of the sea.

Sailing is at its most exhilarating
when the sails are full
and pulses pound. Provided
you stay the course
and ride out the storm.

Don't change direction, based
on a single stretch of
heavy weather.
If what you seek
was near at hand
you would not be sailing.

       –Graves 8/26/11

The Life That You Create

Blame it on the time of day
blame it on your fate.
Blame it on your parentage
or that you were born too late.
The fact, when you come down to it's
not open to debate.
The only life you're going to get
is the one that you create!

     –Graves 11/8/15

The Belly of the Beast

The old foundation crumbles.
Things once held dear
move beyond control.
The strings of puppets stretch
far and away, into a darkness prowled
by monsters.
Rules once dictated by reason waver
and flux beyond familiar form.

The consumption of innocence
proceeds unchecked. A harmony
of dissonance in a fiendishly
scripted meta-plan
too insidious
to be given credence by
gentle people
blindly singing
hopeful hymns
of redemption.

Clarity of insight is roundly
cast as paranoia by
gnomes with hidden intent.
The bugle call of the watch is disregarded.
Its message rejected for "lack of
proper form."

Controllers pivot and spin
like the matador
in the Plaza de Toros, sowing
seeds of docility fertilized by fear
ignoring truth: Caring only
for believability in
the evening-news cycle.

The blood-hungry crowd
cheers the cruelty of the game.
Their voices: Orchestrated instruments in a
symphony spawned of influence
and violence.
The maddened bull charges at
the swirling cape
connecting with nothing
save death.

Poison hides in the communion-wafer
doled out in false generosity
to the indolent.
The lights of the theater have been
carefully set, and focused on
the bare boards of the stage.
Specters dance beyond the edges
of the light to ceremonial music of
the profane transubstantiation. Waiting to
feast on dying souls.

Truth is neither penurious nor kind.
It is merely truth.
It does not pause in pursuit to gather flowers
on a spring morning.
Nor change in the face of malice.
It makes no excuses for the unpleasant.
It does not mask the anomaly.
Truth sees with hard eyes which
brook neither obfuscation nor
fashionably convenient illusion. The choice
that is offered is:
Conform to it
or be cast aside.

At the seeming end – when
all is shaken, and truth

lies in bright, sharp shards
upon the ground. When
integrity serves as the lone
rallying point; a solitary island
in that darkest sea –
take up the shining, razor shards of truth, and slice
and slice again, your way out
from the Belly of the Beast.

Those whose intention was never
to live in the light will
hate you, even
as you are saving them.
You must change the world
from where you stand.
And the light shining into the darkness within
will be seen by others
and will bring them together
one by one
and in the brilliance of the light
those who care to see
will change the world.

–Graves 5/15/15

"Heroes" (To Erin)

I grew up believing in heroes.
I still do.

There are heroes in each one of us.
I know this for a fact.
You may have to dig quite deep
to see that this is true.

And when you do, you'll
recall a time
when a hero's light
shone forth from you
brighter, far than any sun.

Recall how you continued then
when others fell – and you prevailed.
Recall how you held truth above all else
when others fell to lies.
Recall the fight that fell to you
when no one else could see it through.
Recall the times you won.

And if – just now – it's hard for you
to scan the past and see these times
it's not because it never was.
Keep looking – you will find them.

And breathe again a hero's breath
and do those things a hero does.
For you were there when right prevailed.

Be there again.
It's a new day.

– Graves 11/4/16

Runway 24, Lukla, Nepal (The Attainment of Dreams)

To reach the summit of Everest
you must land on Runway 24
in Lukla, Nepal.

There is no other way.

It has a cliff at one end.
A mountainside at the other.
It is only
one thousand
five hundred
feet long.

It is the most dangerous runway
in the world.

But it is the gateway
to dreams.

To reach Everest
you must walk the Khumbu Glacier.
But first
you must scale the death trap that is the Khumbu Icefall.

To earn the chance to do either
you must land on Runway 24.
You must commit.

Runway 24 is the step beyond common reality.
Every prior experience
is shared with those who are content
to live on ordinary ground.

The flight from Kathmandu takes 35 minutes.
The weather changes
quickly.

When the opportunity for flight presents itself
you must take it.
Or remain below.

You must commit.

There is no other way.

The light changes on the summit of Everest
from minute to minute.
No two climbers ever

see exactly the same view
from the height.

As sure as the clouds
of ice crystals rise
on the ragged winds
like a plume
from the summit of Everest

it is there
for the taking.

To attain
you must commit.
You must land on Runway 24.

–Graves 10/2/15

NOTE: The Khumbu Icefall lies at the head of the Khumbu Glacier, on the Nepali slopes of Mount Everest, not far above Base Camp. The icefall is one of the most dangerous stages of the South Col route to Everest's summit. It is estimated that the glacier advances 3 to 4 feet down the mountain every day. Large crevasses open with little warning. The towers of ice found at the icefall have been known to collapse suddenly, sending huge blocks of ice tumbling down the glacier. They can range from the size of cars to the size of 12-story buildings.

This poem is dedicated to those who have landed.

The Mode of the Hummingbird

When you drop it
a stone falls.
It happens.
Your opinion on the matter is not required.

When you blame
your shortcomings on another, you
swear blind fealty to a lie.
You abdicate the dream.
You hand the knife
to the highwayman and lay bare
your throat.
Because this attitude will eventually kill you.

It's harsh.
But it's true.
Like a falling stone.

Those who seek to blind you, or
bend you to their will
will tell you otherwise. It is
their benefit that interests them. Not truth.
If you bend, you become
their marionette.
Jeanne d'Arc can cite you
chapter and verse on this.

At the beginning, nothing
is determined.
Your road does not begin
at it's end.
It does not start in a state
of completion.
It leads not yet to failure
nor to success.

That which you seek to achieve
is there before you.
Waiting.

The hummingbird does not see himself
as small.
He simply sees the world
as large.
And in that mode
he flies.

The limit placed on you
by another
is a lie.
The limit that you place
on yourself
is your chain. It is
the barrier you cannot
surmount.

Unless (of course) you change
your mind.

And when you truly, fully
change your mind
you will find that removing the barrier
is very much like
taking off a coat on a hot day.

After all

the world is
only large.

–Graves 12/9/14

Glossary:

mode: n. 1. a. A manner, way, or method of doing or acting.

Jeanne d'Arc: (Eng. Joan of Arc) (ca. 1412 – May 30, 1431) was born to a peasant family in northeast France. She said that she had received visions from God instructing her to support Charles VII and recover France from English domination late in the Hundred Years' War.

She was sent by the uncrowned King Charles VII to the siege of Orléans as part of a relief mission; and gained prominence after the siege was lifted in only nine days. Several additional swift victories led to Charles VII's coronation at Reims.

On May 23, 1430 Jeanne was captured at Compiegne by the English-allied Burgundian faction. Subsequently, she was put on trial by the pro-English Bishop of Beauvais, Pierre Cauchon on a variety of spurious, politically-motivated charges in an attempt to undermine the legitimacy of the succession of King Charles VII. She was found guilty of heresy and burned at the stake. She was about 19 years old.

Twenty-five years after her execution, an inquisitorial court authorized by Pope Callixtus III examined the trial, pronounced her innocent and declared her a martyr.

Dancing With The Muse

There's something you have to understand
about dancing with the Muse. Nothing

else

can touch
the soul-subsuming exhilaration
of the dance.
Nothing.

But it can also be fatal.

Chat about it with
Hemingway or Poe;
(and a few
hundred others) and they'll tell you:

"The Muse takes
no prisoners."

She will bring you
to places you have never been
then she'll dump you out
and leave you to find your own way back.

And you will sit
and wait for her return
like some strung-out
lover
waiting
by the phone
for a call. And the waiting

will rip out
your heart.

This was Ernie's problem, in the end.
Edgar's, too.
It's no mystery
if you've danced.

When I first danced (truly danced) with the Muse
I never wanted to return
to the world.

She brought me to see things
I had never
seen. Drew out expressions I
had never
before imagined
as she consumed me, bit by bit with
the burning, holy fire.

And she left me
with an empty
craving hunger for creation
like she has with so many others (the whore).

Each of them grateful to be chosen
even while watching the erection
piece-by-piece
of the guillotine
at the end of this road.

The only way to beat the Muse
is to dance with her, and never fail
to lead.
You must drive your art.
You can't let it drive you.

Just because the guillotine is built
does not mean that
your name has been indelibly etched
upon the blade.

She is the most impressive
of the figures of the dance.
For there are truly
"none like [her] among the dancers,
None with swift feet."
None who cause the heart
to Pound.
None who balance quite so well
on motes, drifting in the sunlight shaft
that penetrates the darkened room.

You must lead
and if you do, the Muse will follow
so adroitly that all
you notice is
the lightness
of the pas de deux.

–Graves 10/9/15

Note: The quote "none like [her] among the dancers, None with swift feet." was taken from "Dance Figure" by Ezra Pound

Darkness and Light

First there is darkness.
Until there is light.

Light is not the natural way of things. It is
created. Absent light
the universe is dark.

There is first absence
until you approach.
I feel your warm breath on my neck.
Your presence (as it always does) changes
the essence of my experience. Much

in the way that there is
first cold. Until it is
replaced with heat.

There is inaction before action
status quo before change
stillness before motion.

Prior to hatred there is
the willingness to understand.

We attract that which we fear
because we work to push it away.
In pushing, we must make contact.
And in contacting, we draw it near.

Create, instead, in the direction in
which you would travel.
And the things you fear will
drop away behind you. They cannot
keep up without your help.

The reason that we do not achieve has nothing
to do with anyone else.
Life is as we perceive it and
as we empower it. Prior
to perception, it is not our life.

>				–Graves 4/11/15

A Penchant for Strippers

Life moves like a dancer, lithely wrapping
herself around opportunity with
the fluid grace of flowing time. Beckoning
and teasing in ways as old
as the cold void between the
pulsing heat of stars.

She stirs the hunger that
draws things out of hiding;
squeezing dreams
out of possibility. Anticipation
bred of implication.
Beauty in unanticipated
flashes, in the light
of darkened places.

I've always had a penchant for strippers
so to speak.
Life is like that. I've always
been a bit bemused by
people who are scared
to look at the beauty in life
that is clearly there to be seen
and drink it in.

They look
but with furtive glances. Stares
purposefully averted, as from
a beautiful book on a shelf, never
opened for fear of wrinkling its pages.
A compass, fixed anxiously
on the mundane. Fearful
of leaving the comfort
of the harbor. Not knowing
what now lies ahead.

Michael Graves

The fear of a joy
from which they cannot
withdraw. Joy that may
disturb the calm surface of
their small pond.

Fear that they may have to carry
some new vision, alone. That they
may stumble under the
weight of that load.

Better to not see.

So much to fear.

And all the while
life beckons and whirls, flashing
mysteries to be plumbed; delights
to be seen; wonders to
be unfolded with your fingers
like the fresh petals of the
first bloom in spring.

      –Graves 2/6/16

I am not my chair

I am not the stories
I tell.

I am not the songs
I sing.

I am not the poetry
I write.

I dream
but I
am not my dreams.

I believe
but I
am not my beliefs.

I think
but I
am not my thoughts.

I am not my accomplishments.
They will stand
without me.

I am not my history.
It is a trail
behind me.

I am not my hands.
They are useless
without me.

I am neither the uniform I wear
nor the

causes
for which I fight.

I am neither the car I drive
nor the king
I serve.

I am neither my bones
nor the meat package
in my skull.

The problem with forcing
the answer to everything to fit
into the framework of what is
already known, is
that nothing new
is ever
discovered.

Supreme conceit:
"The Earth
is the center of
the universe."

"Blood flows through
the body because
of tides."

"Man will never
fly."

I learn from my mistakes.
But I am not
those mistakes.

What I have been taught
has changed me

but I am not
those teachings.

I am eternal
and I
do not age.

I am not
my chair.

                –Graves 2/18/17

Why Are We Here?

A friend of mine once said to me
that he wasn't really clear
on the reason behind existence,
on the answer to: "Why are we here?"

Are we here to forge a cleaner soul,
to take our turn at bat?
To wrap ourselves around a pole,
and learn great things from that?

Are we here to learn great truths
and tip the scales to balance true?
Are we here to keep the game in play,
to give Karma something to do?

Are we here to find the perfect match
of fortune and true love?
And to find out after searching
that they rarely go hand in glove?

Are we here to cook the perfect batch
of some outrageous dish?
Or grant a dying child the right
to have his perfect wish?

Are we here to solve deep mysteries
that make the world go 'round?
(If a tree falls in the forest, alone,
does it really make a sound?)

Are we here to differentiate
minutiae from profound?
Or thinking, transubstantiate
our way out of the ground?

And having done so, will it mean much,
as one's life unwinds;
to solve the deepest mysteries,
to find the greatest finds?

Now I suppose, to some degree
these things have some import;
and some of these will give one peace,
if only of a sort.

But really, when the course is run,
how much of it will matter?
See, one might save the universe, or
be trapped by senseless chatter.

To make a choice between these paths;
which one will carry true;
is truthfully the only thing
of value to me and you.

It's not a stupid question, though.
I've given it some thought.
The answer my friend,
to "Why are we here?"
may simply be: "Why not?"

–Graves 2/3/12

Vengeance 'lex talionis' (For the suicide bombers)

The path of vengeance is paved
in blind, smoldering hatred.

A traveled road, lined with damned souls
set to fall like dominoes, one against the other.
It does not end
until all lie writhing in the dust.
A hot, dry wind is all
that remains at the end of this path. A wind
which carries no joy
no satisfaction.

"But the law says: 'An eye for an eye!'
It is only just!"

No.
It is not.

"An eye for an eye" is a crime committed by translators
– in thrall to those thirsting for blood and
for self-serving tumult – translating
for the convenience of those who live to wage death.

The proper reading should be:
"For an eye that is taken, an eye should be replaced."

An eye for an eye.

A life for a life is a far more complex proposition.
It is not true that death, as a solution
is never warranted. But vengeance
begets naught but vengeance.
A repetition of itself, as a round sung
in an unholy song; voiced
in an eternally minor chord.

No life. No happiness.

The appearance of satisfaction, real only to he
whose gaze is fixedly inward.
He who dances alone in his murderous - "I told you so" -
existence.
He is a mote of dust in a barren, soulless
empty land which bears no solace.

You would justify your pain
by adding to the universe, more pain;
you ignorant, self righteously arrogant child!

You would justify your existence by the death of those
into whose eyes you've never looked!

Justice is a more difficult job.
It is not as easy as killing.
Violence is only done where fear is first present.
Vengeance begets only death and vengeance.
It does not balance the scale.

But you knew that from the beginning
and did not care; bearing the rage-fueled seed
which is nurtured only by the compulsion to inflict pain.

If you want true justice:
Get those who created your pain
to understand, and face without denying, the
horror of their acts; and then to make
effective and acceptable amends.
By their own choice.
By their own hand.

                –Graves 2/26/16

Dreams (in four short acts)

Act I:

Your dreams are
your
path

from tragedy
to
joy.

You
decide
to walk the path
or not.

Staying home with
dying dreams
though warm and safe

is tragic.

Act II:

You have never dreamed that
which you cannot
achieve.

And you never will.

This fact
terrifies
some who dream
into disbelief.

It terrifies far more
those who fear

dreamers.

This truth is
as simple

and real

as dust motes
riding sunbeams.

Act III:

Fears:

You create them
permit them and
adopt them
You enshrine them
and worship them.

And that is the

only

reason
that they do not
leave.

It is only your fears
that will stop your dreams.

This has always been
a comfort
to the courageous

and to those who suddenly realize that
they are about
to become

courageous.

Act IV:

Joy is in
your right hand
tragedy
in your left.

Both are already in
your grasp.

                    –Graves 4/30/10

This Moment in Time

You determine this moment in time
no one else.
Its creation is yours.

You conceive it.
You shape it.
You give it life.

Yield the creation of this moment to another, and
you suspend yourself in air
above a chasm
hanging (or not) at their choice.
Your life no longer your own.

Fame, approval, permission granted
by another, may be
taken away.

Except by your own decision
what you create, cannot.

Yield your will to create
and your forward path becomes chosen
at the caprice of another.
The journey bereft of the
joyfulness born of creation.

You create your life
and include others (or not).
You create your future
and include others (or not).

Recall a time you were truly happy.
Wrapped in the arms of someone you love.

Remember a time when you succeeded, and
things were joyfully real.
Remember a time that you won.

These things will be with you, always.
Regardless of what follows.

The creation of joy, of purpose
is within you. It is a gift that you give
yourself.

It is a gift that you share with others, or not.

Build your own life. Create your own dreams.
Live true to your own goals.
Speak your own truths.

None of these can be taken from you.
Unless you first elect it so.

–Graves 4/4/15

Apparency

The tired heart finally sleeps.
The laboring breath stills.
The warm eyes glaze.
And we grieve. The depth of our love
portending the depth
of that gut-wrenching grief, which claws pieces
from the beating heart, shatters life
and changes it forever.

The body fades.
The spirit endures.
Like it or not.

And depth of love, once again
defines the strength of connection.

After the loss, they remain for a time
and grieve beside us, though we
believe them gone: Bound up
as we are, in "seeing is believing."

Perception, though, extends beyond sight.
And sensing their sadness
we sometimes mistake it
for our own.

Belief, however, does not define truth.
Knowing defines truth.
The spirit, it seems, is not necessarily
subject to limits set by pronouncement.

Speak to them and they will hear.
Speak enough, and understanding occurs.
And things change.

I've had these conversations
more than once.
And I have seen things change.

Don't be shocked when you find
that your worst fear
your most mysterious adventure
your most binding chain; turns out not
to be completely as portrayed.

The future does not end
at death.

     –Graves 12/2/16

The Vengeance of Angels

The bright morning belies the peace.
Grasses bend and spin in the fragrant air
on the walk to the sea.
The glory of the morning sun stains
my eyes, hiding with bright fire
the stones in the path.

Any turns – regardless of direction – that form
the road to attainment of the holiest
of causes are justified;
some say.

Malevolence lurks beneath the shimmering
surface of flowing words.
Beneath the surface of the water
a shark waits, hoping
for the smell of blood.

War engenders only hate.
Peace is relative.
In the vengeance of angels, lies
the pathway to hell.

                –Graves 2/13/14

Taking Off My Watch

Taking off my watch
I was finally naked.

No longer bound by time, and the feeling
that finishing
was urgent.

Trees grow
at their own rate.

Love wraps itself around lives
in its own time.

The Earth moves underneath me
at it's own pacing. Why

should I not do the same?

–Graves 6/28/12

Bricks

Believers scare me.

Believers kill people "just because" and
justify it with "they're different."

Two words.
Obliteration of human commonality, in
two words. Like squishing
a bug.

From one's first instant, until
the end; there is this choice:
One can Believe, or
one can understand.

Understanding is the dance
of the expanding mind. Belief
is the blind, determined
fruit of dictates, planted
in stony, shallow soil.

Nothing is understood without perceiving.
Blindness serves only the one who blinds
and his acolytes.

Understanding brings freedom to move
perhaps with ease
perhaps at cost. It is the dance.
Belief is the goose-step.

Blind Belief is a brick baked hard
in the raging fires
of authoritarianism, which demands
adherence and brooks no variance.
Obedience without question is

the mortar which holds
bricks
tightly in
prescribed
formation.

And some prefer that way of life.
I don't.
Some like the ease of life
that comes with never
having to find
the new answer. Bricks

can be anchors in turbulent times.
But they can drag you beneath the surface
of the deep water and pin you there until
you no longer breathe.

From the first instant, until
the end
there is the choice:

One can Believe
or one can
understand.

I continue to try and build windows
in empty space.
And then to open them
and climb out.

–Graves 8/13/15

Circumstance

Circumstances slide against each other
forming situations.
Because that's what circumstances do.
Not entirely unlike tectonic plates
in their action and consequences.

They form ripples, building fluid waves
of opportunity
or condemnation
for being on the right or
the left side of the tide
of general assessment.

In such circumstantial times, the risk is being
burned in the auto-da-fe for seeing
too clearly the State
of the Emperor's clothes, and speaking.
Or for hearing and trying to rescue
the holy songs, drowning in the roar of the crowd.

For heresy or sainthood are determined
chiefly by the mood of the moment. The direction
of the tide. The alignment of circumstance.

Many saints, conveniently presented in witches' clothing
have roasted in the pyre that was lit too soon
so as to hide their holiness;
simply because they were feared.

But what of it?

It happens to us all
I guess
from time to time.

You scare the wrong little people
– the minnows living in shallows, waiting
to be eaten by something –
whose job is not truth, but sales

and they begin gathering wood
and gasoline for the fire
in the service of agenda.

                –Graves 8/21/15

Glossary:

Auto-da-fe: (noun) An auto-da-fé was the ritual of public penance of condemned heretics that took place when the Spanish Inquisition or the Portuguese Inquisition had decided their punishment, followed by the execution by the civil authorities of the sentences imposed. Both auto de fe in medieval Spanish and auto da fé in Portuguese mean "act of faith."

The most extreme punishment imposed on those convicted was execution by burning. As the execution was more memorable than the penance which preceded it, in popular use the term auto-da-fé came to mean the punishment rather than the penance.

"The Emperor's New Clothes": Is a short story by Hans Christian Andersen about two weavers who promise an Emperor a new suit of clothes that is invisible to those unfit for their positions, stupid, or incompetent. When the Emperor parades before his subjects in his new clothes, a child cries out, "But he isn't wearing anything at all!" It has been translated into more than a hundred languages.

Authenticity

No one ever won by believing
in the virtue of tremulous whispers.
By stooping gratefully
before the dripping axe of a scornful king.

Everything that you do etches your presence on the future.
Don't allow your message to be blunted by mice
watching fearfully from the sidelines, wringing their hands.
Or perverted by those cloaked in shadows, leering
as you dance to their terrible music.

Don't do it as "someone else" would do it.
Don't write as you "think a writer should;"
or paint as you "think a painter would;"
or design in fearful conformity to "the rules."

Do things as you would do them with no one to answer to.
Anything else is to live a life of shallow deaths
waiting cautiously for the deep one
which brings your struggling hesitancy to an end.

It's your shot – this life.
Do it right.

–Graves 5/29/15

The Whisper of Sheets

What was it you said?
"I'll stay with you
until the season turns
and then I'm gone."

And I thought:
"Eternity is only
the amount of time
that we possess.
No longer than that, matters."

An entire lifetime
is simply a line of dialog
in a play, set in aeons.
It is the snap of a match, igniting
in the night; its light changing
the landscape in ways
impossible to foresee. Yet
even before the light, we knew
all that the night held.

In the darkness
I feel you breathing.
This temporary eternity is all the time
that I need.

I hear, in the whisper of sheets
a thousand voices
that I have heard
both constantly, for as long as I have been listening
and that I have heard once
and never again. Each
speaking of a separate voyage.
Each voyage a single
life. A discrete path with countless branches

through future.
All of them – and none
of them – with you.

The night looms
long. Empty in the fullness
of space contained
in unpopulated dreams.
And in the darkness
I feel you breathing. I hear again
the whisper of sheets.

This particular eternity is a drop of time.
Temporary, like a handful of rain.

–Graves 11/13/16

Connecting Dots

We live engulfed
by the lower part of the same sky.
All of us.

We breathe pieces of air
which we have shared by proxy
(from time to time)
on a warm Spring day, when the sky held

just

so

many clouds.

We see the crimson afterglow which heralds night
and speaks of things to come. And wonder
what the day has left in store.

We love.

We hold sleeping dreams, until it is time
for them to awake or
to be set free.

We sleep.

We wake – for sleeping can only go on so long
and move (in one fashion or another)
through the day.

We hunger for that which we do not have
(yearn seems such an affected, small word
in this case)
if only in noting its absence.

We relish that which we realize we have. And lose
at some point, that which we do not.

Lines between dots connect us all.
Connect us all.

We die.
We wonder about what comes next.

                –Graves 1/1/15

Catch and Release

Freedom is a supple thing. Agile.
Slippery like a fish in water. Sliding
among wet currents with the ease of belonging.

The potential to set out
to create a chosen effect
and to shape the space and future
created therewith, determines freedom.

You become captive when you hold
so fiercely to intent
that it becomes a thing wrapped in loss and pain
if not achieved.
For in so becoming, it rules you
instead of the other way around.

When the desire to create a specific effect
is gripped too tightly – for too long;
the fingers atrophy and are not
able to painlessly let go and reach
for the next dream.

Bound then, to desperate effort
dreams become anchors. Trammeled channels which
inhibiting other options, dominate
a life otherwise happy
and filled with mutable paths.

Freedom is catch and release.
To exist, it must be catch and release.
And catch again.

–Graves 11/4/15

Note: Catch and Release: The practice – in fishing – of catching a fish and then letting it go without killing it.

Mother is Listening

Stop yourself from speaking
from writing, painting or the expression
of ideas that represent the truth
because it might offend someone
and you stop yourself
because of fear.

Don't call it something else.
Don't try and pretend that it's right.
Or nice.
Because it's not.

Fear is anathema.
It perverts the vision
and mutes the mind.
It wraps the artistic voice in cotton batting.
Ask Picasso about Guernica and
Dylan about Hattie Carroll.
Ask Goya about the Revolución.
Ask them their opinion of the "politically correct."
Ask Mandella about the politics of South Africa or
Ghandi about the benefits of colonialism to the indigenous.
Ask Socrates about the taste of hemlock.

Mute your voice because the truth
sounds offensive to some, and you break
the wings of the soaring bird.
And in that moment
you begin the dance of the death of the soul.

The surveillance culture is rife with
the iconic presence of "Big Brother."
The politically correct, fear
the disapproval of "Mother."

Honesty is born of equity.
Decency is born of courage.

Big Brother is watching.
Mother is listening.
Piss on 'em!

        –Graves 1/23/16

The Poet

I am the poet. I live
the holy nightmare.
I travel the ecstatic transition.

For me, the light bends differently.
The rainbow radiates a vibrant symphony
in the key of red-orange
or some other hue.

Magnificent choirs resound from within
the vast tumble of clouds, hanging in the morning sky
changing with the shifting light.
Harmonically sifting the colors as the sun rises
and echoes brilliantly off the far mountains.

I am the poet. Verse grows
within me, pulsating with life.
Greedy for its own existence.
And forth it comes, skipping gaily or
strutting murderously, as I
in sweet agony of creation, give birth.

I am the poet. A blink
in the wrong direction takes me
to places which are not earthen lands, but
vistas where hope is a particular shade of light.
And rage is a cool breeze on an autumn
afternoon under blazing, red flames of dead leaves.

I am the poet. I see
divinity in snowflakes, and civility
in blood-red rivers of rebellion.

I throb yet, from a love a thousand years past.
And your hot breath across my throat

still haunts me.
And burns.

I am the poet. The ordinary
and the fantastic sit side by side at a table
in a falling raindrop.

A lifetime is lived in a pointed blade
of grass that floats for a moment
on the wind, and then
rushes downstream to rot
on some foreign
shore.

There, to begin again.

     –Graves 11/7/15

Space

You live your life in the space that you create.
Nobody else owns it.
Nothing else controls it.
It is yours. It exists
in tandem with the space
of others.
But it is yours.

You are free to move
or not.
Nothing stands in your way, unless
you elect it so.
(And then it's usually
for some entertainment purpose. One
of the hazards possibly of being
bored.)

It is: As high and wide
as broad and deep, as
filled with light or darkness
as rife with danger or with
sparkling opportunity
as you make it.

And you make it
simply by deciding that it is there.
Before that, it was naught.
After that, it is.

(Too easy, right?)
Light or darkness
mass or absence
matter not.
Up to you.

No one can interfere with it
unless you allow it. Which
you might, from time to time
and perhaps forget that you have;
just for the entertainment value of this.

The: "What!?!? How the hell!!!?..."
of it.
Entertainment. See?
But it is still your space.
And it interacts with
the space of others only
as you decide.

You don't have to believe it.
That's entertainment, too.
Your choice.

You create your life
in your own space.
Nobody owns it.
Nothing controls it
Except you.

And in your own space
nothing stands
in your way.

     –Graves 2/6/15

We Should be More Than Just Entertainment

In a broad sense
we should be more than just
entertainment.

More than figures in the Colosseum arena
scripted parts assiduously assigned.
Movements and motions pre-blocked. Fighting
each other, to the satisfaction
of those with seats.

More than chess-piece
factions, warring
over trinkets.

It is the nature of that being, which
in this state is pretending
to be human, that
we should be so much more.

More than marionettes engaged in games
the outcome of which
was always just part of the plan.

More than the grotesque *bailarin*
who struts and waves the scarlet cape
tumescent with false accomplishment, as he dances
in the bullfight ring with anxiously flaccid pride.
The crowd, like vampires, drawing life
from his pretentious masquerade.

We should be more than this.

More than bread and circuses for
those with seats.
We should be more than just entertainment.

It is the nature of that being, which
in this state is pretending
to be human, that
we should be so much more.

We should be more than
ballerinas dancing on our toes, trying
to please those who would just as soon
see us broken and crawling.

We should be more than entertainment.

                    –Graves 8/28/15

Notes: "Blocking" is a theatrical term which refers to the precise, planned movement and positioning of actors on a stage in order to facilitate the performance of a play, ballet, film or opera.

"Bailarin" (Spanish): Male ballet dancer.

Radiance

In the beginning, it seems just
a bright
light.

Most stars are

content to twinkle;
to politely sparkle
in the cool night sky.

Born sparkling;
that is all
the more to which they
attain.

Other stars
pierce the darkness, with
such

fierce
radiance

that the world is changed.

Brilliance is a natural
quality. Radiance, (as you know)

takes work.

But in radiance
lies the capacity to reach
into the darkness, and

to change the world.

–Graves 8/7/11

Note regarding the subject of the piece: Claude Monet (14 November 1840 – 5 December 1926); is called the founder of French impressionist painting. He painted what he saw; especially in his use of light. He was the most consistent and prolific practitioner of the movement's philosophy of expressing one's perceptions of nature, especially as applied to plein-air landscape painting. The term "Impressionism" is derived from the title of his painting "Impression, Sunrise" (Impression, soleil levant), which is regarded as the seminal painting in the Impressionist movement.

Monet and the other Impressionists fought an intellectual battle against the State-controlled art establishment in France, which at the time considered "French Romanticism" the proper expression of aesthetics in painting. The Impressionists ignored the ridicule of art "critics", the government, and large sections of the public; holding their own showings and continuing to promulgate their vision of a new way of looking at the world artistically.

Currently, The Impressionist School of painting is one of the most popular in the world.

Integrity

No one ever flew by fleeing
from the howling wind.
To fly, the wind must be embraced and flown.
The difference between flight, and flight
is vast.

No one ever captured love
by being someone else.
The difference between affection and affectation
is vast.

No one ever found the unknown land
by pretending to search.
Pretense is a portent of a life of wasted dreams.
The difference between sailing the tide, and remaining tied
is vast.

No one ever grew by being broken to a mold.
Growth requires understanding and the ability to see.
The difference between a lesson and a lesion
is vast.

No one ever tasted freedom, trapped inside a box.
Freedom is an unrestricted leap.
The difference between a vault, and a vault
is vast

Timid Reluctance is a sad little town
of wasted lives, broken chimneys
and excuses.
The difference between prevaricating
and prevailing

is vast.

–Graves 10/23/16

Intention

Your strength is based
on clean intention.
Not clever lines
nor quick invention.
Your ability to exert your will;
and make things right
when the odds seem nil.

It rests on nothing as much, it seems
as your trust in yourself
and belief in your dreams.

                    –Graves 8/21/15

Waiting for You

The flow of time is soft
and silent.

It permeates and
moves. And
does not
stop.

Our sun
at last
softly set
once again.

The spaces between us
filled with darkness.
Until I could no longer
see.

I held your face in my hands. While
the cold night moved
between us, and jealous
in its absence of light
stole yours.

My lungs filled to their brim
with pain
and I sat
alone, watching you. Imagining
your chest moving
with the breath
that never came.

Finally, my lungs emptied
of sound.

Earlier that morning, I had wet a cloth and
carefully cleaned your face.
Not because I had to
but because I
still could.

You spoke to me then
in whispers
of flowers
and of the coming
spring, which
would brighten the woods

and promised

we would again walk the hills
and name the small birds
by their song.

I know that in quiet times
we spoke of the fact that
there is no one living
who has not met another
that they are

certain

they have known
before.

Not a single soul.

But this leap - despite
the number of times I know
that I've lept -
always
seems to be
one of faith.

You and I have danced
this dance
before.
So many times.
From its joyous resume
to its painful end.

This, to me
is as real as the daffodil
in my hand.

I sit now alone, and
wait. Remembering that
it is only
time.

I am waiting for our next walk
in the clean spring air.

The small birds
are waiting.

      –Graves 10/5/12

Life as a Human

The bright orb breaches
the horizon; growing stronger
as it climbs. Sunlight
fades to moonlight
fades to starlight; and again

the sun rises.

That's how it works.

There are some who have been
so metaphysically abused, that
they become offended when they hear this.

Sunlight fades to
moonlight fades to
starlight. And

the sun rises.

That's how it works.

              –Graves 11/25/16

Path

Give one person a tool, and
they will use it
to change the world.

To another, that same tool
is nothing more
than a paperweight.

Decide to accomplish. And in that instant
the path to attainment
lies open before you.

It is there for you to walk.
It's up to you to see the path, and
gather the courage to walk it.

It is there.
But it permits no excuses.
Walk it, or don't.

If you decide to let it pass
don't then fall into regret.
For that will kill you.
Find the next one.

The right path
will pull at your feet.
And the walking of it will be
a dance.

–Graves 2/23/13

Borders is Closing (A Saturday afternoon; and the passing of a friend.)

I will miss the smell of books.
Bound paper. Ink on a page.
And their coffee.

A place to sit, on Pacific Avenue
out of the rain
and write.

It was my version of
Hemingway's "clean, well-lighted place"
(without the despair, loneliness
or nihilistic taint.)

There is something that feels sacred
about a repository of books

for sale or not.

And Borders was one
of the places where
from time to time
I went to write, to peruse
and to wonder at
the thoughts of others.

Stacks of friends-in-paper
of like minds
or not.
A place to go, and touch pages.

To stand in the lighted space, and feel
smooth
paper beneath my fingertips.
And feel the words
of others
in my eyes.

It's not that I mind Amazon
or Kindle or Nook
and the like.
I've shopped the pixel places
but

there is something holy about
"the bookstore"
as an intersection of intellectual
pathways.
A nexus.
A springboard of
dimensional collaboration.

Its occupants were literate.
Thirsty for
words.
Capable of considering
the ideas of another in order to
reach the lofty places – the great open places in
their minds.
Or simply to scratch the itch
of curiosity.

I wonder if the Library at
Alexandria
was like that
before it was sacked.

    –Graves 10/18/14

Michael Graves

The Secret to Good Sex

To seek the grail seems less involved
than the secret to good sex.
Though many seek and seek and seek
and end up as miserable wrecks.
They pen the things that work for them
and end up sounding sappy.
If you want to solve the secret, simply
sleep with someone who's happy.

Sleep with someone miserable, and
you'll end up stained with gloom.
You'll wake in the morning and find that they simply
want you out of the room.
The sex was bad, their life is bad
and you're now the brunt of complaints.
Conveniently, you're near at hand,
though by now you're wishing you ain't.

A train wreck is a joy compared to
sleeping with someone unhappy.
Give it a shot and believe it or not,
your life will be nothing but crappy.
Take this course and you'll live a life
that's laden with regret.
A safer and more joyous game
is classic Russian roulette.

If all you know are happy folks,
it's far less problematic.
Unless, of course, you misconstrue
and they're actually sociopathic.
If you'd care to test my premise and
pursue it to its conclusion,
You'll find that it's an easy one
that results in little confusion.

The answer then is simple and
your life will be quite snappy.
If you just make the person you're sleeping with
exquisitely, delightfully happy.

–Graves 12/30/14

Notes: I kind of "bent" the form of a sonnet in this piece. A Shakespearean or English sonnet consists of fourteen lines written in iambic pentameter, a pattern in which an unstressed syllable is followed by a stressed syllable five times. The rhyme scheme in a Shakespearean sonnet is *a-b-a-b, c-d-c-d, e-f-e-f, g-g;* the last two lines are a rhyming couplet.

Often, the beginning of the third quatrain marks the volta ("turn"), or the line in which the mood of the poem shifts, and the poet expresses a revelation or epiphany.

In this piece there are four quatrains instead of three, the volta occurs in the fourth quatrain, it's written in iambic septameter instead of pentameter and the rhyme scheme is aabb, ccdd, eeff, gghh, ii.

Yes, I bent the form a bit.

The Perfect Life

It's brutal
but it's the perfect life.
Standing up there
on the stage.
Standing out there
in the light.
Taking hearts to destinations
that they've never seen.
Giving them flight.
Music on strings.
Words that sing.
You're giving them
all of them
each of them, wings.
It's brutal
but it's a perfect life.

−Graves 9/5/15

Friendship

Your enemy is not:

Christian
Muslim
Jewish
Hindu
Buddhist
Shinto
Sikh

He is not:

Palestinian
Israeli
American
Russian
Chinese
Japanese
Iranian
Indian
Pakistani

There are differences between men.
That makes them interesting.
That gives them something to talk about.

Your enemy is the specific man
who would use these differences
to breed distrust, and then
carefully
fan that distrust into hatred.

That man plants seeds that
he has carefully gathered from his own
hatred.

He is a man who knows
no peace except death.
For him, there is no sunny laughter of children, only
the sound of young recruits to his cause.
And his cause is death.

He dances like the matador, inflaming
the bull with deception
and pain, to the point
that it cannot
think.
It charges anything that moves.
He leads it to death.

Nothing more.
He knows that
there is no gain
at the end of his road.

There are differences between men.
That is what makes them interesting.
They share similar dreams.

This man dreams of
setting them at
each others throats. He
is enemy to them all.

Children play in green fields
in the warm afternoon.
He watches from the tree line, hidden
among the weeds. Plotting
ways to turn them into creatures
of hate.

Every country
every religion
every race

has these men.
The war is: All
of us, against the few
of them.

All of us.

            –Graves 9/19/12

On the observation of a cripple, yet buoyant.

The body is bent
the spirit is not, and pulls it
like a child dragging
some favorite blanket
from place to new place
looking for delicious candy.

–Graves 9/9/15

Different Doors

Art is a competitive event
only among fools.

Do not concern yourself with those
who create what you do not. No matter
the brilliance of their light.
For they do not create
as you would create.

There is no competition among artists.
There are only different doors.
Other roads.
Windows that open
onto a different land.

The world that you create
is yours. And its vistas
are like no others.

Share it
or not.
It is your decision.
And only yours.

Do not be concerned
that what you create
will be less than that
of another – or more.

For in that direction lies
only death; or worse:
the decision to not create.

You are born of the raging winds
the mirrored pool

and the winding road that never ends.
You reside in that highest place
that looks out on vistas
which only you can see.

You are the only one
who will bring them home.
Or not.
As you decide.

        –Graves 8/7/15

A Poet's Wish

A life in service of the Muse; spent
planting dust from imaginary stars
in fecund, conceptual earth, from
which grows poetry like the
twisting vines of clustered, climbing roses.

For that, it seems
is pretty much how it's done.

A life in which passion's burning
blood is the most tepid
to which one aspires.
And from that blood fall drops
of glowing fire, along the winding road.

Spots of light, to guide a traveler
too long locked in search.
Spots of light for me to follow on that
darkest night and find
my own way home.

A life which ends
in sunset spilt like shining blood
on western skies.
A night which with her cool
sparkling blessing
bids both farewell to one
and joyous welcome
to another day.

                    –Graves 4/16/16

The Secret Handshake from God

Don't give me this
about writers block!

Just start!
Start anywhere!
Just write!
There is ALWAYS more to write!
There is no shortage of pixels;
of paper
of blood for ink.
Just poke her! and you'll
wake the Muse.
Write! and she will respond to the calling. All
hot and trembling.

You see! You do! – LIFE
is the grist.
It's ALWAYS changing;
refracting differently.
Always a new angle.
Always a new angel.
Always a rift opening
in the pattern that
catches the eye
of the mind.

WRITE! Damn it! Paint! Compose! Sing!
What are you waiting on?
The mighty acknowledgment?
The secret handshake from God?

I think not...

–Graves 8/11/12

The Taken Road (with gratitude, to Robert Frost)

I may have mentioned this before
but there are times in life, I think
when every poet wonders if
the road not taken, might, perhaps
have been the psychopath.

Yet, paths being – obviously – what they are
he wonders to himself how far
he'll be allowed to run the road
he's chosen for himself, unbowed.

And when at some point time's embrace
becomes impossible to elude in the chase
will its arms be icy cold or hot?
Though, in the end it matters not.

For with each new beginning, there's always been
as plain as day, an earlier end.
And no matter the times we've run this road
from end to end
it always (always) seems new and strange
when we set foot on it once again.

–Graves 6/12/15

Weaver (for Taylor Newton Stewart)

You weave, and the music swells.

Waves of textured sound, each
a thousand pieces of fractured glass
turn transcendently smooth in the woven interaction.

Each note

as clearly individual as raindrops

falling through open sky.

Musical phrases join to form aural images:
Of the flight of a soaring bird;
the pain throbbing from an angel's harp;
broken glass on a dusty basement floor.
Of torrential rain in tumultuous air; swelling
to fill every
aspect of space.

I hear this in your music.

Melody like the flight of a sparrow
carving a twisting, turning path, fast as lightning
through the cooling air of a huge barn
in the fading glow of an ebbing sun.

I hear the blade of grass pushing aside
dark loam in an empty field.
I hear the raging wind driving waves of sand
across the face of an ancient rock wall.

I hear the melody of time, bending

around a corner

in the dark.

I hear this in your music.

I hear the chords made by clouds
drifting slowly in a rainy sky.
I hear musical notes falling in syncopation, like rain, cooling the
thick, sultry night; merging
in swirling resolution as cleanly as

moonlight slicing

through dark

freezing air.

Poetry is carved
from ancient things.
It is chiseled from discarded pieces of time.
Images of what is, and what has
never been, moving with distinct direction.

Music is woven.
Fluidly crafted from that essence
which comprises universes. Vibrations
woven upon the loom of form.

Infinitely fine threads, balancing minute
variations, each determining the fate
of all the rest.

The fire that you form fuels the spirit of man.
It falls to you, the task of drawing music
from that which, left alone, are naught
but plain and simple sounds.
Yet, when woven, ignite the fires of dreams.

I don't know how you do it.
I just listen.

–Graves 4/15/16

Sequential glossary:

Musical phrase: A musical work is typically made up of a melody that consists of numerous consecutive musical phrases; each phrase having a complete musical sense of its own.

Syncopation: Syncopation is a general term for an interruption or disturbance in the regular flow of rhythm in a musical or other piece. It is used in many musical styles. It is used in many ways, but in the form of a back-beat, syncopation is used in virtually all contemporary popular music.

The Easy Answer

Okay, let me get this straight.

You start with a really
really big, sterile rock
spinning in space.
It's got smaller rocks.
It's got water, heat
light and dark
It's got gases surrounding it.
It's got no life.

Then, over a very, very long time
this pile of sterile chemicals racing through space
(no dirt, because dirt requires vegetation
and it's got no vegetation)
combines and recombines in
every possible combination of the available
rocks
water
heat
atmosphere
light and dark.

Mind you, there is no starter mixture
like you need for a good sourdough bread
or yogurt or kefir or a nice cheese.
There's no decaying organic matter from a forgotten
compost pile or stagnating swamp (there's nothing to stagnate).
None of that.

And what you're telling me, is that
over hundreds of millions of years of
sterile stuff, plus
sterile stuff, plus

sterile stuff
you get a really big rock spinning through space
covered with intelligent life – to say nothing
of a myriad of other, wildly divergent
life forms?

And you get this
with no outside interaction of any sort?

That's like saying, "If all you have to work with
are 1's and 0's and you stack them together in an
infinite array; at some point you are going to
spontaneously get a 3 or a 7 or a 9."
Because you happen to have a 3 or a 7 or a 9
and you think you're going to look bad
if you can't explain how it got there.

Here's a similar question:
If you dumped a million sterile marbles a day into
a lifeless ocean. How long would it take
for Leonardo da Vinci to
come striding forth from the waves;
to just come walking out of the ocean
...surfboard in hand?

Does it seem like there's
something missing in this equation?
I'm not necessarily saying it's God
and I'm not necessarily saying it's not.
It's just that there has
got to be something else
going on here. You
can combine all of the dead chemicals that
you want, and you're not
going to get something that's alive, Okay?

It's a lazy, clueless approach.
And it disingenuously, conveniently leaves out

the fact that life
does not come from non-life.
Life comes from life.

It's like having an F5 tornado run through a huge junkyard of scraps, and leave behind a working airplane.

It's an easy answer.

—Graves 6/13/15

Barriers to Flight

Icarus could not fly.

Until he decided that he would.
So it was, with:

The Wrights, at Kittyhawk
who did what others had not.

And Charles
on fixed-wings, speeding
across the icy, dark Atlantic sky
under shining, white stars.

And Amelia
riding the whipping wind. Soaring
high above the wide
wide
blue Pacific.

And Neal, Buzz and Michael
in the silent, hot lunar dust.
All eyes fixed to the sky.

And the Others...

The barrier to flight, is the belief
that flight is impossible.

Believe strongly enough
and it will be.

"Impossible." Covers a multitude of sins.
For such is the abandonment of a dream.
And there are few, more damaging sins
than leaving dreams to die.

Heads have been beaten bloody against
brick walls for not realizing
that the wall
is not the real barrier.

Before Icarus decided to fly
he could not.

If you are thinking to yourself:

"...and look what happened to Icarus."

That's why you can't.

>   —Graves 3/4/16

Why we do what we do

We create.
In order to grasp a clearer sense of that
which stretches out behind.
And from this sighting, spot
those points which help us plot
a course along the path which lies ahead.

And what is this trip, but
sensation and adventure? What is life, but
a search for realization and amazement
among the round, gray rocks
of an eternal seaside? An
entertaining side-trip into a realm
where we imagine ourselves as not
all-powerful and omniscient?
We create.

If you wait for the Muse
to bequeath you your gift
what you desire will never arrive.

We create.
If, along the road, you see
the diamond of your dreams, it's up to you
to draw it close
or pass it by. It's your diamond.
Why should it matter
to anyone else what you do with it?
Until you do with it
what you will.
And upon that, for someone else
may rest everything.

We create.
The future

lies only in the realm of magic.
For nowhere else is it to be found.
It is only as
you create
it. And how else
would you describe magic?

Naught but memories inhabit the past.
Nothing living to be found there.
You may as well search the eyes
of those you see along the way
for the ghosts of lovers who have
long since left the room.
Many do. And live lost in the search.

We create.
We dance on metaphysical toes
across a very personal universe.
We do what we do
for love of the dance.
And for the entertainment.

      –Graves 10/18/16

Actors

We are
all of us
actors upon the spherical stage, who
have agreed to remember to forget
that we are more.

We have agreed to not
know why the dance takes place.
So that we may know - each time - its sparkling joy
as if it were something new.
Something experienced for the first time.

We have agreed to wear the costume
and to live the play.
To play, and ring the curtain down.
Applause or not. Curtain call
or not. Because the opportunity
to play, is all.

We play the part, and spin the
shimmering web of creation.
All of us.
Some just remember to forget
better than others.

–Graves 10/18/16

Notes: "Ring the curtain down": (theatrical idiom) To lower a theater curtain, usually at the end of a play.

Curtain call: A curtain call occurs at the end of a performance when the actors return to the stage to be recognized by the audience for their performance. In a musical performance that went particularly well, it usually involves the performance of an additional song in response to the enthusiastic applause of the audience.

Barriers

Between here
and success are barriers.

For them to make any difference
you first have to
see them as barriers.
And then you have to believe
that they can stop you.

It's pretty simple.
And if you're accustomed to barriers stopping you
it can seem unavoidable.
And stupid to think otherwise.

All things outside of yourself
that seek to stop you
you can surmount.
If you decide to.

Seriously. And
if you don't believe this, that's
a great example of a barrier.

You just have to become
bigger than the barrier.

A barrier is an excuse to turn back.
It's an acceptable response to fear, that you
can buy-into without looking
bad to others, because:
"Well, it was just too difficult."

Sure.
Give up.
No one will think

less of you.
"No one could have done it."

Of course; you could
have done it: If you'd gotten
brighter in your approach
tougher in your pursuit; or
if you'd refused to quit.

A barrier is a reason to remain
comfortably bound by the familiar.
It can also be an excuse to avoid attainment.

For, to end the game by winning
is nevertheless to end the game.
And without the game, what's
left to do?

There's a difference
between a barrier
and the wrong path.
The wrong path was
wrong from the start.
The right path is one in which you believe
and always have.
You know it's right
daunting or not.

"It's always darkest just before the dawn."

Astronomically, not true.
The saying comes more from
the observation of barriers. And
their relationship to
persistence and success. In truth, it's
actually darkest around 2:00am.

Barriers often appear to be
most insurmountable
just before they fall.
Ask anyone
who has achieved goals.
It's true.
To surmount barriers requires persistence, and
maybe a different approach.

A barrier is an odd form of entertainment.
It is the oldest form.
And the most basic:
You create barriers in order
to find out whether you can best them
and win, despite them. Because
if you just went out and won all the time
where's the fun in that?
It gets mind-numbingly boring after a while.

If you thought about barriers differently
you would ignore them and
just succeed.

Simple, really.
But, so is life.

$\quad\quad\quad\quad$ –Graves 4/15/16

Back story: Somewhat ironically, the power in my house went out this morning (5/5/13 – the date of the first draft of this piece) at 9:00am; shortly after I started this piece. I completed it in the dark. Just thought you might find that amusing.

Sailing (Song of the Daemons*)

The hull of my boat is painted blue.
We moor sometimes to clouds.
Eon to eon we've sailed the summer
winds into autumn and back again;
riding the raging storms of winter
into the passionate arms of spring.

Our tides are the golden sunset
and the fiery red of dawn.
We ride the cool, black pre-dawn winds
soaring the broad remnants of sky
between the ebb of moonlight and
the sparkling of the stars.

Sometimes, on a calm spring day
or blustery autumn afternoon
we'll lie-to off a cloud bank
and watch life unfold below.

You might have felt us watching
felt a presence where no presence was.

That was us
or maybe not.

You might have felt the unexpected
breath of air, one dead-calm day.

And known
without quite knowing, that
it was us, passing by.

The movement out the corner of your eye
that makes you turn your head

to see nothing but the crystal air
was us.

Or maybe not.

We course the currents below the storm
and above the raging sea.
It's we who send the dolphins out
to foundering ships

sometimes.

We spare the fleeing refugee.
We wake the pilot mid his flight.
We send the rains to quench the fire.
We cause the ticking bomb to fail.
We turn the tide when all seems lost

sometimes

We tip the scales a bit, because
you strive when others might lose hope.

And as you do
we pause to intervene.

Sometimes.

–Graves 12/12/14

*Daemon: noun, Daemons are good or benevolent nature spirits; beings of the same nature as both mortals and gods, similar to ghosts, spirit guides, forces of nature or the gods themselves (see Plato's Symposium), unlike the Judeo-Christian use of demon in a strictly malignant sense.

I used this term not because I was describing daemons, per se, but because it was the term that most closely described the hero-beings who are the subject of this piece.

Terrorist

The cat watches birds.
As long as he stays inside
we have no dispute.

                –Graves 3/10/11

The Cliff

It is inevitable.
None escape.

For each soul, the nature of the cliff is unique.

A dark crag shrouded in thick, wet fog
towering in a windy sky.
A massive precipice overhanging
a gray, unfriendly sea.
A looming, vertical face of jagged rock
glazed by freezing rain.

You will scale it
or you will not.
You will best the fear
or you will fail.

The premonition of dire consequences
wearing down your concentration;
the wavering self-doubt, bound to your soul with fear
like the grip of an iron hand.

To the degree that they exist, you
have created them.
To understand that this is so;
is the first step in ascending the cliff.

You will win most often, only
after you realize
that there is no reason that you need to fail.

Before that point, failure looms like
massive, hungry jaws
drawing you in, against your will.

Michael Graves

Realize for yourself
that there is truly
no reason that you must fail;
and you will break its grip.

        –Graves 3/3/16

The Dance

We are
each of us
an individual viewpoint
of creation.

We are
each of us
a Creator-in-disguise.
On vacation from the "big job."

We are dancers
of the eternal pavane. Indulging

in a casual pirouette
to spin
a galaxy on its way. Or
a playful
tour en l'aire
to remind the planets how it's done.

Working out
the choreography of a
freestyle jazz routine
on the head
of a pin;
with the rest of the angels.

We dance.

We weep.

We sow joy.

We inspire.

We dance: Trailing songs

and the poetry of a million lives lived.

–Graves 12/14/12

Glossary:

Pavane: A stately court dance by couples that was introduced from southern Europe into England in the 16th century.

Pirouette: A full turn of the body on the point of the toe or the ball of the foot in ballet

Tour en l'aire: (French: "turn in the air"), in ballet, a complete single, double, or triple turn in the air.

Woman

Too often man lives doomed. In love
with beauty alone. An image
woven in sensation, expectation and
delight. Composed of equal parts: vibrant thoughts and
immortal expectations. Like
some wondrous, conjured creature sprung
full-grown from sorcerer's brew:
A dash of impossible
a pinch of unattainable, simmered
in unimaginable beauty
brought forth before the shining moon
to wander Earth for him alone.

Bereft, he lives
unable to paint into reality
the portrait, large enough to
encompass the scope of his imaginings. Never
realizing that the sweeping size
of his expectations
is far
too
small

and far
too
over-thought
to fit
the truth which
awaits him
should he but see
what is there
and
what is not
and

in comprehension, begin
by saying, simply, "Hello".

The only hope that he has
is to not die before
realizing that worlds beyond splendor are his
for the taking, should only
he grasp
this single concept.

    –Graves 10/3/14

The Root of Strength

Complexity is a Siren's song, which
haunts the labyrinthine path.
It is the spawning seed
which births the lies that
hold the world in thrall.
Infinitely fragile constructs
susceptible to toppling by
any who simply look
and see.

The world ends
for those who will not;
just beyond the edge of the familiar.
It ends at the whisper which
casts doubt upon the way that
they were instructed to believe.

For beyond that point
is blindness. And
the terrifying void.

You fashion your potential;
your personal universe, so-to-speak
and your destiny
from that which you decide
to see and understand.

For that which you understand
you may control.

Or not.

As you choose.

In the simplicity
of understanding
you will find the root
of strength.

$$-\text{Graves } 5/29/16$$

A Simple Step

If you want
to change the world
then your path is simple.
All you must do
is change
the world.

Nothing more.

                –Graves 6/30/12

Quality (for Don Dewsnap)

There are many who settle
for the cards that they're dealt.
Content to gnaw whatever bone
lands on their plate.
Content to live the quiet, secure life.

There are fewer who seek
to better their lot.
To push harder. To accomplish
what others will not – sometimes
dare not, do.

They begin with a decision.
With tools and a purpose.
A canvas and a vision.
A chart that ends in the middle of an ocean.
A conjecture wanting for resolution.
With naught but a goal and
perseverance. And the drive to take it
beyond where before it ended.

They begin with what is.
And form it into what can be.
They start with who they are.
And make themselves into what they would be.
They take "cannot"; and transmute it
by alchemy of will, into "can".

And upon these few
everything
depends.

–Graves 9/6/15

Spiderwebs and Evolution

Why do spiders all
make their webs exactly
the same way?

I mean, there is no
red-brick spider-school they go to
where they sit in rows and attend
design classes.
Right?

No instruction manual issued:
Some ancient, dusty tome passed down through generations
on how to structure a web.

No seminar, workshop, website (sorry)
nor blog.

God? Whispering
secrets to each
individual spider?
I would think
that he/she/it has
better things to do.
No...
I don't think so.

How is it that they
all know how to build webs?
So that they ripple
in the breeze, just so
like glistening, silken
banners of some alien civilization?
Or hold firm, like
cracks in a shattered
pane of air?

How is it that they know
how to cross the
staggering distances
to the opposite anchoring
point? How to string them above the
ground?
How to link together
each
strand, so that they
each
serve their appointed structural task?
So that they don't tangle
collapse, and wind up
a snarled, silken heap?

Instinct?

Instinct – I think – is the simple
stock answer for people
too stupid or too
cursory to admit that they have
no idea.

DNA?
Who/what programmed it?
Sounds a lot like "instinct."

Why do spiders
all make their webs
the same way?

Well, ALL spiders probably
don't make their webs
exactly the same way.

But a lot of them
a WHOLE lot of them
do.

I wonder why this is?

And evolution...

Life evolves.
But why?

Evolution posits
Life forms changing
(due to survival advantages) over
millions of generations so that
they can survive better.

It sounds reasonable.
But

the math doesn't
seem to work.

A change happens in one gecko.

A flash of mutation. And maybe
that gecko survives better.
And maybe he (or she)
doesn't get eaten by a bird
stepped on by an elephant
swallowed by a fox or smashed
by a falling branch.

One gecko.

And even if he does survive
it's only

one gecko

out of millions
(of the old-model gecko).

The gene pool it seems, would – by
mass of sheer inertia –
favor the old-model gecko.

It's like a crapshoot.
And, eventually all crapshoots
crap out. By dint of numbers.
The house wins.
The "usual" prevails.

I'm not so much a "creationist"
necessarily

but it seems like Darwin missed a variable
or two
in the equation.

And it seems like
(since he'd already "done the math") that
"people" (as many people do) went along with it.
Because it sounded good, and they
didn't want to do the math.

So what is the answer?

I think the real answer is:
"Re-check the math."

Spiderwebs and evolution.

Tip of the iceberg.

—Graves 6/6/15

Note: In case you were wondering: Geckos have the ability to run up walls, but it's not because their feet are sticky. Geckos have two billion, spatula-tipped filaments per square centimeter on their toe pads. Each of these filaments is only a hundred nanometers thick. This makes them so small that they interact at the molecular level with the surface on which the gecko walks, tapping into the low-level van der Waals forces generated by the fleeting positive and negative charges of molecules in the surface that the gecko is climbing. And their feet are constructed so that this gripping ability works in just one direction.

Slicing Tomatoes

I love slicing tomatoes.
Big, ripe, red ones.
Or heirlooms: Striped and colorful;
dense and juicy.

The knife needs
to be sharp, though.
Sharpen the right knife, and
slice them into paper-thin
moist, red pieces.

The secret is to let the knife
slide. Don't push it.
Let the knife do the work.
Slide it. And it slices right through
the firm, red
juicy
meat
of the tomato.
Let the knife do the work.

A lot of things are
like slicing tomatoes.

                –Graves 6/12/15

Tips From My Father

My father was an engineer.
He gave me tips along the way.
He told me, "Work while you're working, son
and play when it's time to play."
He said, "They'll wonder after you
and ask which way you went.
If, in every job you do, you give it 110 percent."

–Graves 1/7/16

Note: This piece is dedicated to my father: Douglas C. Graves. The best man I've ever known.

Thanksgiving

Today, I am thankful.

For the rocky coast; the
challenging wind; the
circumstance that
makes me grow.

For the stars
which bid my vision
up and out.

For family, who warm my way
guide my steps
and make me a little
crazy, sometimes.

For friends, who
sweeten my life
with affinity.

For the one that I've
finally found, who
brings my life full circle.
And for falling in love
all of those times before.

For the child, who wakes
in the clear morning light
and is not afraid to see.
Who dresses the future
in dreams; and
graces the world
with wonder
and possibility.

Messages in a Bottle

For those who make the music, that
fills up spaces in booming
joyous abandon or peacefully sings
the sparkling stars to sleep
in the night sky.

For the poet
whose words blaze with dreams that
inflame imaginations, kindle passions, stoke
the heat of life; and who paints with
rippling colors in the imagination
the road that takes us where
we have not been.

For the painter
whose vision spans the distance
between each of the separate
viewpoints of mankind
and joins them as one.

For the song defiantly sung, despite
suppression, and for those with
the courage to carry
the tune.

For those who walk
the lonely road
and keep the peace.

For the seekers of truth
and the dreamers of dreams
who return with visions
that seed the future.

For the clear, strong voice
which bends back lies with
simple truths, and drives out evil

like chaff before the summer wind.
That voice which vows to
never accept defeat.

And I am thankful for
those who come back.

They who are the
unstoppable
children of the wind.

And I am thankful
for those who share these thoughts.
Whoever you are
in whatever land
by whatever tongue
in whatever time.

For we share the same path.

—Graves 11/19/15

Decision

The dream does not exist, which
has not in its conception, come
coupled with challenge
as its birth-twin.

Alike, no wish exists
that in its forming thought is void
of gauntlet thrown
to make it so.

Life concatenates
challenge to challenge.
That's what makes it
Life.

To wake and dress, or drink
hot coffee
without spilling.

To ascend
the vertical rock face
ice-covered
in a live, raging
gale. Or to fall

into hopeless
riotous love, never
to be the same. Ever.

Life concatenates
that is

what makes it
Life.

Michael Graves

The path was void before you came
win or lose
you decide which fork to walk.
And you
alone.

Who refuses this, is soaked too deep
in need to blame, his head
too thickly bound in batting
to hear the holy
songs.

You
and you alone decide:
poison or
life.

The dream does not exist, which
has not in its conception come
coupled with challenge as its birth-twin.

Delight or
poison.
you decide.

–Graves 12/24/10

America 2197

You are not what you once were. Nothing
is.
Life changes. Life
evolves. Life
encompasses. Or life
dies.

Where once you lounged, cloaked
in alabaster privilege. Steel
ribbons stretching edge to
edge, binding
east to west. Sleepless
fires in your massive coal forges spewing
forth your iron might.
You now sing

the tight, electric harmony.
Photons eclipse electrons.
Cloud surmounts earth.
Lines, long ago fallen before
the ubiquitous Net have been carried away
like pruned canes in a
vineyard now out of season.
Your roots have lengthened
and mingled, drawing life from the ends
of the spherical Earth.

You scan the far horizon with
Viking eyes; fiercely blue
fearing nothing.
The cold wind strews your flaming
Scottish hair and you smile
the knowing smile of one
certain to win all.

On the night air, your sweet Arabian lips call my name
with cool aplomb and draw me close
murmuring tales of the Rub'al-Khali.
Of Dubai, before
the oil came
to your new home.
The sultry breeze whispers against
your smooth skin: Ebony silk
in the quiet morning of this new day. The cruel
uphill fight to attain, attain, attain
now so old as to be
legend. A curio
on a bracelet of charms.

Your voice dances in my ears
my sweet Parvati, and whets
all of my senses.
The gods of ancient Dwarka speak
through your fingers, and weave the future.
The ancient navigators of
Micronesia, now plot courses past
the stars with ease.
The sea was, after all
just practice.

The tango of the Argentine
speaks in your blood, and cries out
for the inevitable conquest.
Your breath quickens at the scent
of opportunity, for you are one
not without the fiercest of passions.
The view from the peaks of Aconcagua and Chimborazo
king and queen of the Andes
has sharpened the acuity of vision
that you bring to your new home
to the point that the hawk - not the eagle - is jealous.
For you too now share the aerie.

You are as unstoppable
as the unkillable
persistence of your
beautiful Russian forebears.
As transcendently enduring in the face
of adversity as the ancient monks
of the Tibetan high plateau. Of
the pilgrim looking toward Mount Kailash
from Idaho.

You are so much more than you were.
And so much less than you will be.
My love.
My America.

—Graves 2/12/15

Notes:

1. Rub'al-Khali: The Rub' al Khali or Empty Quarter is the largest sand desert in the world, encompassing most of the southern third of the Arabian Peninsula. It includes most of Saudi Arabia and areas of Oman, the United Arab Emirates, and Yemen. The desert covers some 250,000 square miles.

2. Parvati: Parvati, also known as Gauri, is a Hindu goddess, nominally the second consort of Shiva, the Hindu god of destruction and rejuvenation. Generally considered a benevolent goddess, she also has wrathful incarnations such as Durga and Kali. She is the gentle aspect of Mahadevi, the Great Goddess, with all other goddesses being her incarnations or manifestations.

3. Dwarka: Dwarka is a city and a municipality of Jamnagar district in the Gujarat state in India. Also known as Dwarawati in Sanskrit literature, Dwarka is one of the seven most ancient cities in the country. The legendary city of Dwarka was the dwelling place of Lord Krishna.

4. Aconcagua: Aconcagua is the highest mountain in the Americas (22,837 feet). It is located in the Andes mountain range, in the province of Mendoza, Argentina. It is one of the Seven Summits.

5. Chimborazo: Chimborazo is the highest mountain in Ecuador (20,564 ft). While Chimborazo is not the highest mountain by elevation above sea level, its location along the equatorial bulge makes its summit the farthest point on the Earth's surface from the Earth's center.

6. Mount Kailash: A peak in the Transhimalaya range in Tibet. It is considered a sacred place in four religions: Bön, Buddhism, Hinduism and Jainism. Tibetan Buddhists call it "Kangri Rinpoche" meaning "Precious Snow Mountain". Bon texts give it many names: "Water's Flower", "Mountain of Sea Water", "Nine Stacked Swastika Mountain". For Hindus, it is the home of the mountain god Shiva and a symbol of his power symbol "Om"; for Jains it is where their first leader was enlightened; for Buddhists, it is the navel of the universe; and for adherents of Bon, it is the abode of the sky goddess Sipaimen.

Stardust

We are the creators of infinite dreams.
Each of us.

Yet many work so very hard
to attain that hollow acclaim
which comes with being
little more than meat.

A hamburger.
Wrapped in a GMO-laced bun
with mustard and onions.
And maybe some fries.

The holy end-game, little more
than the accumulation of trinkets. And
the universal in-and-out.

Which (in the scheme of things) is
no more than an entertaining pinball machine
plugged into a wall sitting in a corner
at one end of a vast realm of Magic.
A vast realm of Magic.

The stars are dust compared to us
they shine in the void of space.
Bright lights in the sky, creating nothing.

We are the creators of infinite dreams.
Gods wrapped in delusion.
Shuttered by amnesia.
Made idiots by distraction with baubles;
tiny, twinkling, glittering baubles.
Mumbling confusedly in a darkened room.
Playing inconsequential games
with broken fingers.

Michael Graves

The only thing;
the only acceptable resolution to this
is to turn the tide.

We are the creators of infinite dreams.
Each of us.
We are so much more than stardust.

–Graves 9/5/15

Maniac (for Syria)

The morning is soft and
wet with stained
dew among the fallen.

The black birds are circling below
the clouds
awaiting the feast.

You have already forgotten the day
and plot the night; hungry
for justification.

The innocent impaled.
The defenders left rotting;
turning the field fecund for your hollow posturing.

We marched on them
caught up in the call. Our pay laced
with the promise of ribbons. But

there is no honor in killing
children. No glory in the death of
civilians waiting simply for the cessation of noise.

The small white dog walks
the fields and digs
his nose into the fresh morning earth. And

the truth now fills us
who are left, with shame. Though remorse
in excess, is paid with death.

We raise our voices, and
the new arrivals focus hard on the horizon. Seeing
fevered visions of heroics.

Their heads high with
determination. Imagined validity, in
the seamless glory of an unchallenged purpose.

Their step springs with green.
The spring, to them is a time for games.
And so it is.

For they have not yet seen death.
Nor smelled the blood that fouls
the roses of delusion.

You expect us to run
into the guns for you.

I will not run
into the guns for you.

     –Graves   4/28/16

On Poetry and Social Responsibility

Poetry is one of the most dangerous, most powerful, and one of the most unorganized forces in the world.

Consider the effect that a single poet can create on the human psyche.

Shakespeare, Rumi, Rimbaud, Dylan, Poe, Pound, Dickinson, Baudelaire, Cummings, Neruda, Yeats, Plath, Ginsberg, Burns, Bukowski, Dylan Thomas, Blake, Frost, Wordsworth, Whitman, and countless others.

Poetry combined with music was powerful enough to play an important part in helping to change the social face of my country in the 1960's. If you were there to witness it, you know exactly what I mean. One of the most famous pieces of poetry of that decade begins: "How many roads must a man walk down/before you call him a man..."

Poetry soothes the aching heart. It kindles the flame of love. It is a precursor to inspiration. It calls men to sail a sea that they otherwise might not. Poetry performs a catalytic function between conditions: a bridge between disassociation and engagement; between non-involvement and responsibility; between denial and consideration.

At some point, a piece of poetry left a mark on you that was indelible. You still can recall it. That quality in poetry can bring change to the world – literally.

If poetry is not also used to bring about needed change in social and political conditions, it denies a fundamental aspect of its basic purpose, and to this degree and in this way, it lies fallow.

Poetry is not bound by physical barriers. It is not stopped by walls. It can infiltrate elitist compounds, and pierce the walls of fortresses and prisons. It can bypass embargoes as easily as a breeze travels down a city street. I am writing from a redwood forest in California. You are reading this. Distance is not a barrier to poetry.

One of the reasons that poets are held in contempt by those who use force to suppress, is that while poets command the very, very real skills to inflame the spirit of those who are oppressed and move them to active social change or even open, violent revolt; that ability is far too often used by poets for nothing beyond introverted maunderings, voiced in cautious, hushed, whiny tones. As a result, suppressors find spitting on poets a very safe thing to do.

Poetry is powered by the human spirit. It is carried in the hearts and minds of the people. Historically, ideas have toppled empires. All social movements – all of the changes in history – have been sparked by communication.

"...I am the song on the lips
of slaves.

I am sire to the million whispers in the night;
before the riotous dawn.

I am the throbbing life blood;
the hope that breathes yet, beneath the heel
of the iron boot.
And awaits its time.

And I am that time
which *will* come.

I am the driver of men, beyond broad, deadly
expanses, thirsting
for new worlds.

I am the line
plotted past the edge of charts.
I am the dreams beyond those
yet dreamed.

I am the new voice of songs yet
to be formed on the lips of
those yet to be born.

And I am the dawn
of a new Age..."

Poetry once lacked the proper distribution system. We now have a distribution system which is more powerful than any in the history of Earth – the Internet. Change can now potentially take place "one reader at a time" on a very, very broad scale. Poetry does not need to sway six billion people in order to achieve its goal. It only has to reach and affect those with significant influence, or reach a significant number of people, for change to occur.

What if we had a million poets creating life-changing pieces in a wave which is directed at a single point of oppression? Or directed at a focused, few points of suppression? Think about it. What kind of effect might we then create?

It is time to send the tyrants screaming into the night, pursued by a wave of voices that no number of bullets can ever kill.

Poetry can change the world. But only if it is wielded, not proffered. Get organized. Pass it on.

"Night Must Fall on the Regime"

The time has come.

Night must fall on the regime.
The summer air half a world away is filled
with the screams of souls that you have betrayed.
You, whose proper function is to serve.

You, who turn your country on the roasting spit of oppression,
charring humanity to black flakes over
the painful fires of violence; seasoned
with the smell of fear.

This is *not* the way of humanity!

You do *not* speak for me!

You could once commit your perverted crimes shrouded in secrecy.
But now, worldwide
awareness of your atrocities is just a URL click away.

The video taken with the phone of
the man in the street – upon whose neck
you once could stand with impunity
– and posted to the web, makes

secrecy no longer your option.
No longer your shield.

To sit silent and do nothing while you continue, degrades me
and stains each of my brothers and sisters with shame.

To permit you to persist, reduces the humanity of each one
of the inhabitants of Earth.

Each one.

This is NOT the way of a leader.

This is *not* the way of humanity.

A populace is NOT your collection of personal toys
to be played with, and bled!
You pathetic, wanton child!
There is no pride in this.
Only decrepitude.

Stalin was thus.
Hitler was thus.
George III was thus.
The Masters of the Inquisition were thus.
These are your brothers-in-spirit.

If the only reasoning that you will respond to
is a knife at your throat,
then consider that you are now on notice.

Messages in a Bottle

Your lies and deceit will birth the bloody tumult.

I weep for your countrymen.
I weep for my brothers and sisters.

It is time.

Night must fall on the regime.

I am the poet.
And I live in a billion minds.
We are the dreamers of dreams.
And we will prevail.

Your remains will blow away on the fresh winds of morning
before the rising sun of a new day.

There are a million voices waiting to take my place.
A million songs being honed.
A sky-full of razor-sharp arrows that are all aimed at your heart.

Our songs live in the minds of your people.
Our songs form the million whispers in the night
before the riotous dawn.
Our songs feed the throbbing life-blood of hope
that breathes yet beneath the heel of the iron boot.
Awaiting its time.

And that time has come.

For the sake of humanity.
For the sake of songs yet to be formed
on the lips of those yet to be born.

Night will fall on the regime.

You cannot dull my advance.
Your suppression only sharpens
my quill and broadens my legend.

We live as one unturnable wave of forward motion.
And we speak for humanity.

We will outlive you.
We will outlast you.
You who would crush all hope.
You are my enemy.
This is personal.

I am the singer of songs.
I am the dreamer of dreams.
My brothers and sisters and I inspire the future, and craft
the inspirational blade that even now thirsts for your throat.
There are more poets on Earth than you can count.
And more than you can ever crush.

You cannot stop us.

The time has come.
Night *will*
fall on the regime.

–Graves 2/11/15

Author's Note: Though this piece was originally written about poetry, its premise applies to all forms of art and the artists that power them. We are all in an unprecedented position to influence not only our culture, but the combined cultures of the planet. And who better to do it? Politicians have been wearing this hat for millennia and have driven themselves as a group into a generally distrusted and despised condition of existence. It is only fitting that we, as artists, bypass and handle. Not as those who would govern the culture, but as those who illustrate the direction that a culture should properly take in its evolution from the existing scene to a more ideal scene, and provide effective encouragement and motivation for the achievement of that evolution. As artists, it's our job and should be our united purpose.

About The Author

Michael Graves is a West Coast Poet who lives in the redwood covered mountains just outside of the San Francisco Bay Area. His unusual approach to poetic subjects spans the spectrum from the cerebral to the deeply erotic and has won the hearts of thousands of readers. *"Messages in a Bottle: Communications to My Future Self"* is a collection of 67 of his most popular poems.

Graves writes from a sometimes gritty metaphysical point of view which evokes the resilience of the human spirit. "Many poets weight the reader with their feelings regarding the futility of the human condition. I've chosen not to do that. My poetry speaks to the potential of the human spirit and its ability to prevail in the face of adversity. My aim is to lift my readers, not burden them. I've have been told on more than one occasion that the affirmative nature of one or another of my pieces has saved a life."

"As a beginning poet, I started writing poetry in self defense in high school in order to stay awake and survive a math class," Graves says.

"It wasn't until I took a poetry class with James Doyle in the mid-1970's at the University of Northern Colorado, that I began to understand quality as it relates to poetry. Among other things, Jim helped me to see that if I couldn't express an idea in a way that was different than it had been said before, why bother? Around that time I began the process of growing up as a poet. I owe him a lot in that regard.

"Most people who read poetry want the truth to reach out through the words and grab them by the throat. They're looking for a portal through which to escape the mundane. My hope is to provide that for my readers."

www.ingramcontent.com/pod-product-compliance
Lightning Source LLC
Chambersburg PA
CBHW022106040426
42451CB00007B/143